Introduction

. . . "It is written: 'Man does not live on bread alone, but on every word that comes from the mouth of God.'" (Matthew 4:4)

Many of Jesus' teachings were centered around a meal. We join together as Christians for communion, so what better way to get a child's interest than through food? *Cooking With Christian Kids* is the perfect way for children to learn about God and his love for us as they create a wonderful variety of delicious foods. Children will learn the basics of cooking and will practice valuable math skills and other skills like following directions, fine motor skills, critical thinking, and many more. You will see self-confidence build as the children create and serve, give away, or feast on such delectable goodies as Wonder Bars, Mock Apple Pie, Clouds of Heaven, and Sand Tarts, to name just a few.

Each recipe features a Bible verse and discussion starter to provide you and the children with some "food for thought." Read the Bible verse with the children and help them relate it to their own lives. Then discuss the situations, stories, or discussions presented to help the children grow in their understanding of God and his love for us. (Note: The Bible verses featured on the recipes are in chronological order of the Bible to enable you to easily choose a verse to accompany a lesson you are teaching.)

The variety of recipes presented enable children of all levels to enjoy "cooking in God's love" with or without a great deal of adult assistance.

Dedication:
This book is dedicated to my mother and father—the first two cooks I knew, and to my friend Tess whose help was beyond compare.

Before You Start . . .
1. Read through all of the safety rules and information on pages 2–5. Discuss with the children why the rules and information are important. Make a copy of them to display in the cooking area.

2. Show the children how to measure something correctly—measuring exactly to the designated level.

3. Show the children how to assemble electrical equipment.

4. Show the children how to turn the stove on and off.

5. Let the children practice cracking eggs.

6. Show the children how to test if something is done (for example, poking with a toothpick, piercing with a fork, seeing if something has pulled from the side, etc.).

TS-CQD-075

D1447775

Basics You Should Do

1. Always put long hair up.
2. Wash hands with antibacterial soap and continue to keep them clean while cooking.
3. Roll up your sleeves and get any loose clothing out of the way.
4. Never lick your fingers and continue cooking or take a taste off of a spoon and then return the spoon to food. This spreads germs.
5. Always work on a clean surface.
6. If cooking with meat, fish, eggs, or poultry, wash all utensils, plates, cutting boards, knives, faucets, knobs, and countertops completely with hot water and antibacterial dish soap before using again.

Cooking Basics

1. Always have an adult present when using a source of heat for cooking.
2. If you are cooking, be sure to read the recipe for the oven temperature and turn the oven on before you start working through your recipe so that the oven will be preheated.
3. Always have hot pads available.
4. Always turn the handles of pots to the center of the stove so they won't get bumped and spill.
5. Keep spills cleaned up as you work so you don't slip and fall or work in a messy area.
6. Be sure to remove spoons from pans when stirring something that is cooking.
7. Turn off the burners or oven when done cooking.

Hot Liquids

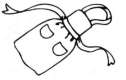

1. Boiling liquids will burn! Always have an adult present when boiling any liquid.

2. If asked to stir a cooking or boiling food, be sure to hold the pan with a potholder in one hand and slowly stir with the other hand so as not to splash the liquid.

3. Always keep your body clear of the stove.

4. Whenever you are cooking, you must keep an eye on what is cooking so that it doesn't burn. Be sure to use the correct temperature.

5. All boiling liquids produce steam that can burn.

Using Knives

1. Knives are dangerous! Always have an adult present when using knives.

2. Always use a cutting board.

3. Never use a dull knife.

4. Hold food firmly on the cutting board with fingers well out of the way of the cutting blade. Then move the knife slowly and carefully, holding the knife with the blade down and gripping the handle of the knife with all four fingers wrapped around the handle and the thumb on the opposite side of the handle for balance.

5. Always hold the knife by the handle, never by the blade.

6. Never put a knife into a sink of dirty dishes where you may not see it when washing.

7. Always pay attention to what you are doing while cutting.

*8. When using a potato peeler, always peel away from you.

Using Electrical Equipment

1. Have an adult show you the proper way to use electrical appliances.
2. Make sure all loose clothing is confined while near electrical appliances.
3. Always keep electrical appliances away from water and the sink.
4. Keep your hands dry when working with appliances.
5. Never put an electrical appliance into a sink full of water to wash.

Using a Blender

1. Assemble the blender before you plug it in. Unplug it when you are done and before you disassemble it.
2. Always keep the lid on when the blender is in use.
3. Never try to stir anything when the blender is on.
4. Never fill a blender to the top as the liquid inside surges to the top when turned on.
5. Never put your hand into a blender—there are sharp blades in the bottom.

Using a Mixer

1. Assemble the mixer before you plug it in. Unplug the mixer when you are done and disassemble it.
2. Never try to scrape the sides of the bowl while the mixer is running.
3. Never put your hands into the mixing bowl while the mixer is on.
4. Add ingredients slowly to the mixing bowl to allow the mixer to do its job.
5. Never pull the beaters out of the bowl while they are still moving.

Things to Do Before Beginning

1. Read the recipe all the way through.
2. Collect all the ingredients needed.
3. Collect all the materials needed.

Things to Do After You Are Done

1. Put away all the ingredients.
2. Put away all materials used.
3. Wipe off counters and sink.
4. Sweep floor of any crumbs.
5. Make sure all leftovers have been put in proper containers.
6. Make sure all electrical appliances have been turned off.

GP275508 Cooking With Christian Kids

Seven Days of Creation Salad

God saw all that he had made, and it was very good . . . (Genesis 1:31)

God is the ultimate creator. He gave each person the ability to create: to draw, to write, to sing or play music, to invent. What is your creative outlet? How do you use your talents to give thanksgiving to God? Read Genesis 1–2:3 to learn about the gifts God created and gave to us.

Ingredients:

lettuce

celery

carrots

peas

mayonnaise

Parmesan cheese

bacon

eggs

(Amounts can vary according to size of bowl.)

Materials Needed:

strainer

clear, deep bowl

spoon

cutting board

knife

pans

skillet

paper towels

Directions:

1. Cook peas and let cool. Cook bacon and let cool. Pat off excess grease. Cook hard-boiled eggs and let cool.

2. Wash and pat lettuce dry. Rip lettuce into small pieces. Place in the bottom of the bowl to form the first layer.

3. Cut celery into small pieces to form the second layer.

4. Cut carrots into small pieces to form the third layer.

5. Place the cooked and cooled peas on top of the carrots to form the fourth layer.

6. Spoon mayonnaise on top of peas to form the fifth layer.

7. Peel and slice eggs and place on top of mayonnaise to form the sixth layer.

8. Break bacon into small pieces. Sprinkle on top of mayonnaise to form the seventh layer.

9. Sprinkle Parmesan cheese over the top. Chill and serve.

6   GP275508 Cooking With Christian Kids

Garden of Eden Salad

The Lord God took the man and put him in the Garden of Eden to work it and take care of it. And the Lord God commanded the man, "You are free to eat from any tree in the garden; but you must not eat from the tree of . . . knowledge . . ." (Genesis 2:15–17)

From the beginning, God provided for our needs and expected us to obey his rules. He gave man a free will to make choices with. What choices do you have to make?

Ingredients:

2 bananas, grapes, strawberries, ½ of a watermelon, pineapple chunks (You can use any combination of fruit except apples!)

Materials Needed:

bowl, can opener, cutting board, butter knife, ice cream scoop

Directions:

1. Use the ice cream scoop to scoop watermelon balls until you get to the shell. Place the watermelon into the bowl. Save the watermelon shell for later.

2. Peel and slice the bananas into the bowl.

3. Wash the strawberries and cut off the tops. Add them to the fruit in the bowl.

4. Open the can of pineapple chunks and pour off the juice. Add the pineapple to the fruit in the bowl.

5. Pluck the grapes off the vine. Wash and add them to the fruit in the bowl.

6. Mix the fruit and pour it into the watermelon shell.

Adam's Apples

When the woman saw that the fruit . . . was good for food and pleasing to the eye, and also desirable for gaining wisdom, she took some and ate it. She also gave some to her husband, who was with her, and he ate it. (Genesis 3:6)

Things we are not supposed to do are often tempting to do, but in the end, this is harmful to our well-being. Can you name things that are a temptation to you?

Ingredients:
Rome apples

red cinnamon candies

Materials Needed:
baking dish

apple corer

potato peeler

spoon

Directions:

1. Core the apples.

2. Peel the apples one inch from the core apple hole.

3. Place the apples upright in a baking dish.

4. Fill the center of each apple with red cinnamon candies.

5. Bake in a 375-degree oven for 40 minutes or until tender. Spoon cinnamon syrup from pan over the apples several times during the 40-minute cooking time.

GP275508 Cooking With Christian Kids

Eve's Apple Blush

. . . "I heard you in the garden, and I was afraid . . . so I hid." (Genesis 3:10)

Have you ever been afraid? What are some things that could scare you? How do you overcome your fears?

Ingredients:

4 cups apple juice

one 12-ounce can apricot nectar

½ cup lemon juice

¼ cup grenadine syrup

one 12-ounce bottle cold ginger ale

one pint lemon sherbet

Materials Needed:

pitcher

punch bowl

ice cream scoop

measuring cups

Directions:

1. Combine juices and grenadine syrup in a pitcher and chill.

2. Pour chilled juices into a punch bowl.

3. Carefully pour the cold bottle of ginger ale into the punch bowl.

4. Scoop sherbet balls and place them in the punch.

Noah's Rainbow Cookies

"I have set my rainbow in the clouds, and it will be the sign of the covenant between me and the earth." (Genesis 9:13)

Rainbows are a promise to everyone on earth that God will never again destroy the earth and its inhabitants because of the sins of people. What promises can you make to God?

Ingredients:

2 ¼ cups sifted flour

¼ teaspoon salt

2 teaspoons baking powder

½ cup margarine

½ cup granulated sugar

½ cup brown sugar

2 eggs, beaten

¾ teaspoon vanilla

1 tablespoon milk

5 colors of food coloring

Materials Needed:

mixer

bowl

measuring spoons and cups

cookie sheet

hot pads

wax paper

knife

Directions:

1. Mix margarine and both sugars. Add eggs, vanilla, and milk.

2. Mix the dry ingredients together.

3. Add the sifted mixture to the creamed mixture, blending completely.

4. Divide the dough into 5 equal balls. Color each dough ball with food coloring.

5. Roll the dough into five snakes. Pat the snakes flat.

6. Lay the snakes one on top of the other, pressing down to make them stick together. You should have 5 colors of layered dough.

7. Roll in wax paper and refrigerate overnight.

8. Slice the layered dough in ¼" sections and form into a rainbow.

9. Bake on ungreased cookie sheet in a preheated oven at 375 degrees for 7–10 minutes.

GP275508 Cooking With Christian Kids

Tower of Babel Tortillas

. . . *"Come, let us build ourselves a city, with a tower that reaches to the heavens, so that we may make a name for ourselves . . ."* (Genesis 11:4)

People are always trying to impress each other with "material things." Can you think of something that you have that you like to show off? What would God want us to be "showing off?"

Ingredients:

tortilla chips, refried beans, lettuce, tomatoes, onions, shredded cheddar cheese, black olives, sour cream, salsa, guacamole

Materials Needed:

cutting board, knife, pan, plate, spoon

Directions:

1. Chop tomatoes, onions, and lettuce.
2. Heat the refried beans in a pan.
3. Lay chips on the plate. Spread refried beans on chips.
4. Put a layer of tomatoes, then onions, then lettuce, and then cheese on the chips.
5. Add guacamole, sour cream, and black olives. Top the tower with salsa.

Rebekah's Well Cake

"Before I finished praying in my heart, Rebekah came out, with her jar on her shoulder . . ."
(Genesis 24:45)

Faith is praying in earnest and believing your prayers will come true. Have you ever prayed and then received what you prayed for? Have you ever prayed and not gotten what you prayed for? Why do you suppose God did not answer your prayer the way you wanted?

Ingredients:

3 cups flour

2 teaspoons baking soda

2 teaspoons baking powder

1 teaspoon salt

2 cups sugar

⅓ cup cocoa

2 cups cold water

1 teaspoon vanilla

2 teaspoons vinegar

¾ cup cooking oil

Materials Needed:

9" x 13" pan

sifter

bowl

measuring cups and spoons

fork

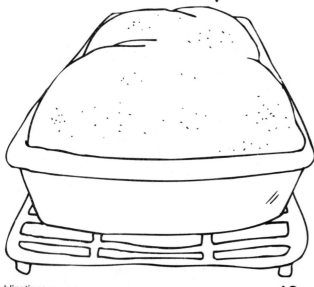

Directions:

1. Mix all dry ingredients together and then sift them into the ungreased pan.

2. Dig three "wells." (Scoop out three holes in the pan.)

3. Put vanilla in the first hole.

4. Put vinegar in the second hole.

5. Put cooking oil in the third hole.

6. Pour cold water over the whole pan. Mix with a fork.

7. Bake at 350 degrees for 40–50 minutes.

GP275508 Cooking With Christian Kids

Jacob's Dream Cake

He had a dream in which he saw a stairway resting on the earth, with its top reaching to heaven, and the angels of God were ascending and descending on it. (Genesis 28:12)

In the Bible, dreams were thought to give people an insight on things. Do you ever dream? What are your dreams about? Do you think dreams are helpful?

How many instances can you find in the Bible in which God revealed his will through a dream? One example is Genesis 28:12. Can you find more?

Ingredients:

Crust
3 cups pretzels
2 sticks margarine

Filling
1 stick margarine
1 teaspoon vanilla
1 pound confectioners' sugar
2 eggs

Topping
4 bananas, sliced
20 ounces crushed pineapple, drained
12 ounces Dream Whip™
chopped pecans
maraschino cherries

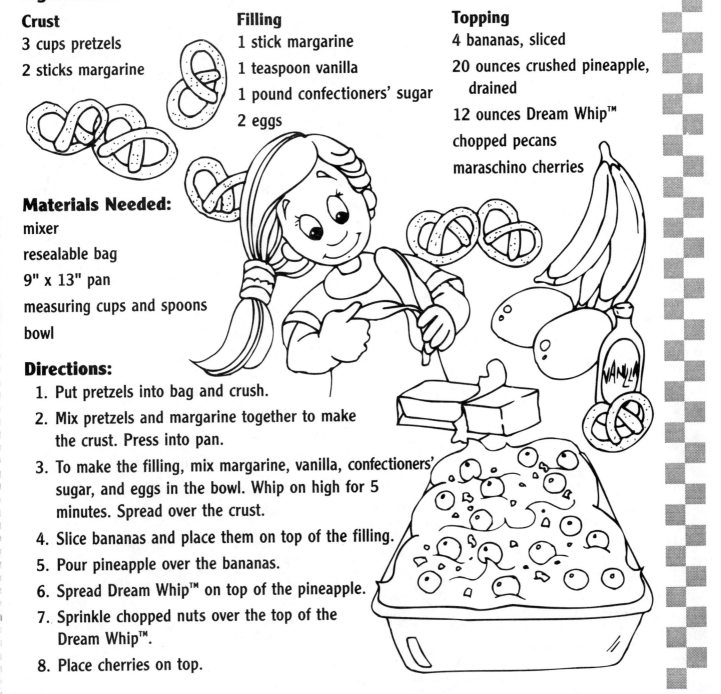

Materials Needed:
mixer
resealable bag
9" x 13" pan
measuring cups and spoons
bowl

Directions:

1. Put pretzels into bag and crush.
2. Mix pretzels and margarine together to make the crust. Press into pan.
3. To make the filling, mix margarine, vanilla, confectioners' sugar, and eggs in the bowl. Whip on high for 5 minutes. Spread over the crust.
4. Slice bananas and place them on top of the filling.
5. Pour pineapple over the bananas.
6. Spread Dream Whip™ on top of the pineapple.
7. Sprinkle chopped nuts over the top of the Dream Whip™.
8. Place cherries on top.

GP275508 Cooking With Christian Kids

Reuben's Pie

When Reuben heard this, he tried to rescue him from their hands . . . (Genesis 37:21)

The story of Joseph is one of family love and jealousy. Have you ever felt jealous of a brother or a sister? Can you love someone and also be jealous of him or her? Find out how love is described in 1 Corinthians 13:8.

Ingredients:

9" unbaked pastry shell

4-ounce package shredded Swiss cheese

2 ½ ounces sliced corn beef

½ cup sauerkraut, well drained

2 tablespoons flour

¼ teaspoon salt

a dash of nutmeg

2 eggs, beaten

1 cup half-and-half

Materials Needed:

strainer

measuring cups and spoons

mixer

bowl

fork

Directions:

1. Prick the bottom and sides of the pie shell and bake at 425 degrees for 7 minutes.

2. Shred beef and then sprinkle it on the bottom of the baked pie shell.

3. Sprinkle cheese and sauerkraut on top of the beef.

4. Mix well the flour, salt, nutmeg, eggs, and half-and-half.

5. Pour mixture over the ingredients in the pie.

6. Bake at 325 degrees for 35–40 minutes, or until set. Let sit 10 minutes before serving.

GP275508 Cooking With Christian Kids

Honey Spice Butter

Then their father Israel said to them, "If it must be, then do this: Put some of the best products of the land in your bags and take them down to the man as a gift—a little balm and a little honey, some spices and myrrh, some pistachio nuts and almonds." (Genesis 43:11)

Have you ever received a gift from someone who came from far away to visit you? What would be the best products you could take to someone if you went far away on a trip?

Ingredients:
whipping cream

honey

cinnamon

nutmeg

fresh bread

Materials Needed:
clean baby food jars with well-fitting lids

measuring spoons and cup

knife

tape player and tape

spoon

Directions:
1. Fill several baby food jars with whipping cream. Put the lids on tight.
2. Turn on some music and let the kids shake the jars in time with the music.
3. When butter (curds) separates from the watery liquid (whey), your butter is done.
4. Drain off whey. Combine butter from several children to get ½ cup butter.
5. Mix in 2 teaspoons honey.
6. Mix in ½ teaspoon cinnamon and ⅛ teaspoon nutmeg.
7. Spread on a warm slice of bread.

Angel in a Bush Treats

There the angel of the Lord appeared to him (Moses) in flames of fire from within a bush . . . (Exodus 3:2)

The Lord uses unique ways to get our attention. For Moses, it was a burning bush. Can you think of ways the Lord tries to get people's attention today?

Ingredients:

angel food cake

coconut

sweetened condensed milk

Materials Needed:

cutting board

knife

two bowls

cupcake pan

Directions:

1. Cut the angel food cake into cubes, approximately 2" x 2".

2. Pour the sweetened condensed milk into a bowl.

3. Pour the coconut into the other bowl.

4. Roll the angel food cake in the sweetened condensed milk and then in the coconut.

5. Place the "angel in a bush" pieces in the cupcake pan.

6. Bake at 350 degrees for 15 minutes or until the coconut is lightly browned.

Milk and Honey Shake

So I have come down to rescue them from the hand of the Egyptians and to bring them up out of that land into a good and spacious land, a land flowing with milk and honey . . .
(Exodus 3:8)

Do you ever wonder what it would be like to have everything—all the food, clothes, land, houses, and cars you could ever want? Do you sometimes get sad seeing what other people have and wonder, "Hey what about me?" Then it is time for a reality check!

When was the last time you missed a meal or had only one outfit to wear day after day after day? God has blessed most Americans with a land of milk and honey. Look around. How can you help the less fortunate in your community?

Ingredients:

½ cup milk

2 teaspoons honey

½ banana

½ cup orange juice

¼ teaspoon vanilla

3 ice cubes

whipped cream

Materials Needed:

measuring cups and spoons

blender

glass

spoon

Directions:

1. Peel banana.

2. Pour milk, honey, banana, orange juice, vanilla, and ice cubes in the blender.

3. Cover and blend for one minute or until smooth.

4. Pour into glass. Top off with whipped cream.

Red Sea Slush

Then Moses stretched out his hand over the sea, and all that night the Lord drove the sea back with a strong east wind and turned it into dry land. The waters were divided, and the Israelites went through the sea on dry ground, with a wall of water on their right and on their left. (Exodus 14:21–22)

The Red Sea was parted by Moses so the Israelites could escape from Egypt. Can you imagine walking through the Red Sea? What do you think it would sound like? What do you think it would look like? Could something like this happen today?

Ingredients:
1 cup frozen strawberries

½ banana

small container strawberry yogurt

1 cup orange juice

Materials Needed:
blender

cups

measuring cup

Directions:
1. Put all ingredients in the blender.
2. Turn blender on medium for 2 minutes or until ingredients look completely blended.
3. Pour into cups and enjoy!

Vegetables Aplenty

We remember the fish we ate in Egypt at no cost—also the cucumbers, melons, leeks, onions and garlic. (Numbers 11:5)

The Israelites complained about being free because they didn't have the same foods as they had when they were slaves. Do you ever look back on a past experience and think, "Wow! Those were the good old days!" when in reality, it was a very tough time?

Ingredients:

1 cup sour cream

2 teaspoons dried minced onions

1 teaspoon dried dill weed

a shake of salt

a shake of garlic powder

vegetables: cucumbers, carrots, cherry
    tomatoes, broccoli, and cauliflower

Materials Needed:

bowl

mixer

measuring cups and spoons

potato peeler

knife

tray

Directions:

1. Empty one cup sour cream into the bowl.

2. Mix onions, dill weed, salt, and garlic powder with the sour cream to make the dip.

3. Chill in refrigerator.

4. Wash, peel, and cut vegetables. Place on a tray around the bowl of dip.

GP275508 Cooking With Christian Kids

First Fruits Cake

Present a cake from the first of your ground meal and present it as an offering from the threshing floor. (Numbers 15:20)

God gives us his best. Who do you give your best to?

Ingredients:

1 can crushed pineapple

1 can cherry pie filling

yellow cake mix

1/3 cup chopped walnuts

1/4 pound butter

Materials Needed:

9" x 13" baking pan

can opener

cutting board

knife

Directions:

1. Dump the can of pineapple and pie filling into the 9" x 13" pan.

2. Dump the dry cake mix over the top of the fruit. Do not mix.

3. Sprinkle walnuts over the top of the cake mix.

4. Slice one stick butter into 1/8-inch squares and spread over the top of the nuts.

5. Bake at 350 degrees for 30–35 minutes or until golden brown.

GP275508 Cooking With Christian Kids

Aaron's Almonds

The next day Moses entered the Tent of the Testimony and saw that Aaron's staff, which represented the house of Levi, had not only sprouted but had budded, blossomed and produced almonds. (Numbers 17:8)

All things are possible with God. The Israelites doubted Moses. They doubted God's promise, and so God sent a sign for them to see. Do you sometimes need a sign to be reminded of God's faithfulness?

Ingredients:
1 cup blanched almonds

2 tablespoons butter

1 teaspoon salt

½ teaspoon nutmeg

Materials Needed:
shallow pan

paper towels

measuring cups and spoons

spoon

Directions:
1. Place almonds in the shallow pan with butter.

2. Place the pan in a preheated, 350-degree oven. Cook for 20 minutes, stirring occasionally.

3. Remove from oven. Drain on paper towels.

4. Sprinkle salt and nutmeg over nuts and toss.

Super Strength Stew

. . . The Spirit of the Lord came upon him in power . . . (Judges 15:14)

God gave Samson strength. He also promises that we can do all things with God who strengthens you. How does God strengthen you?

Ingredients:

1-pound can carrots

8-ounce can whole potatoes

8-ounce can green beans

8-ounce can corn

¼ cup all-purpose flour

1 envelope dry onion soup mix

3 cups cut-up, cooked beef

Materials Needed:

can opener

large skillet

spoon

one-cup measuring cups

bowl

Directions:

1. Drain vegetables into a bowl, saving the liquid. Pour the liquid into the 1-cup measuring cups. You will need a total of 3 cups of liquid. (If you do not have enough liquid, just add water to to the vegetable liquid to get the required liquid.)

2. Combine flour, soup mix, and liquid into a large skillet. Mix well.

3. Heat to boiling, stirring constantly.

4. Stir in vegetables and beef.

5. Cover and cook over low heat for 10 minutes, or until heated through.

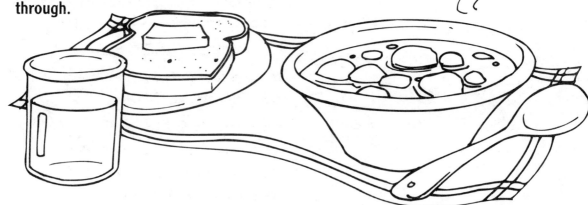

Comfort Bread

. . . "Refresh yourself with something to eat . . ." (Judges 19:5)

People look for comfort from food, a soft blanket, a hug. Where do you find comfort?

Ingredients:

12 slices white bread

soft butter or margarine

cinnamon

10-ounce jar preserves (your favorite flavor)

4 eggs

2⅔ cups milk

2 tablespoons sugar

Materials Needed:

measuring cups and spoons

8" x 8" baking dish

knife

cutting board

fork

non-stick spray

bowl

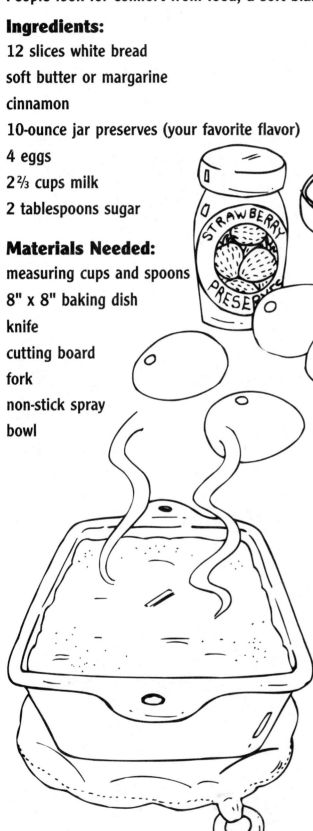

Directions:

1. Preheat oven to 325 degrees.
2. Cut the crust from the bread.
3. Spread butter on one side of each slice of bread.
4. Use non-stick spray to grease the baking dish.
5. Arrange 4 slices of bread, butter side up, in the bottom of the baking dish.
6. Sprinkle lightly with cinnamon.
7. Spread preserves over the bread. Repeat, making two more layers.
8. Mix eggs, milk, and sugar with a fork.
9. Pour over the bread and bake for one hour or until a knife inserted in the center comes out clean.

GP275508 Cooking With Christian Kids

Harvest Wheat Biscuits

Now the people of Beth Shemesh were harvesting their wheat in the valley . . .
(1 Samuel 6:13)

During harvest time in the Bible, everyone from infants to elders went to the fields to help. It was a community effort. Can you think of times when your community comes together?

Ingredients:

1 cup biscuit mix

¼ cup whole wheat flour

½ cup plain yogurt

2 tablespoons honey

Materials Needed:

bowl

spoon

cookie sheet

non-stick spray

measuring cups and
   spoons

Directions:

1. Mix biscuit mix, whole wheat flour, honey, and enough yogurt to moisten the dry mix.

2. Drop dough by the spoonful onto the greased cookie sheet.

3. Bake at 450 degrees for 8–10 minutes or until golden brown.

GP275508 Cooking With Christian Kids

Commander Cheese Calzone

Now Jesse said to his son David, "Take this ephah of roasted grain and these ten loaves of bread for your brothers and hurry to their camp. Take along these ten cheeses to the commander of their unit . . ."
(1 Samuel 17:17–18)

When armies went to war in Bible times, their families often brought them meals. That way, the families were able to keep up on the war and the health of their family members. How do you keep in touch with loved ones? How do you show you care?

Ingredients:

refrigerated pizza dough

1 cup shredded cheddar cheese

1 cup mozzarella

½ cup ricotta cheese

¼ cup Parmesan cheese

spaghetti sauce

Materials Needed:

bowl

spoon

baking pan

foil

non-stick spray

Directions:

1. Spray non-stick spray on the pan. Spread the pizza dough in the pan in a ¼"-thick circle.

2. Stir the cheeses together in a bowl.

3. Sprinkle the cheese on half of the circle of dough.

4. Fold the empty side over the top of the cheese side and pinch the edges closed.

5. Bake at 400 degrees for 10 minutes, uncovered.

6. Cover with foil and bake for another 8–10 minutes.

7. Top with spaghetti sauce.

Morning Sunrise Sandwiches

"The God of Israel spoke, the Rock of Israel said to me: 'When one rules over men in righteousness, when he rules in the fear of God, he is like the light of morning at sunrise . . .'" (2 Samuel 23:3–4)

When people are sad, we often say that they are "blue." When people are excited, we often say that they "sparkle." When people are good, we often say that they "shine." Can you think of a time when someone you know was like the light of the morning at sunrise?

Ingredients:

bologna, egg, milk, salt, pepper, slice of American cheese

Materials Needed:

measuring spoons, non-stick spray, skillet, muffin pan

Directions:

1. Spray non-stick spray in the skillet and fry bologna until it curls up at the edges.
2. Spray non-stick spray in the muffin pan.
3. Place fried bologna in the muffin pan. Press down to form a cup.
4. Crack an egg into the bologna cup.
5. Pour 1 teaspoon milk over the top of the egg.
6. Sprinkle with salt and pepper.
7. Bake at 375 for 15–20 minutes or until egg is cooked.
8. Place a slice of cheese over the top and put back in oven for 30 seconds.
9. Remove your sandwiches from the pan and enjoy!

Individual Cheesecakes

Elijah said to her, "Don't be afraid. Go home and do as you have said. But first make a small cake of bread for me from what you have and bring it to me, and then make something for yourself and your son. For this is what the Lord, the God of Israel, says: 'The jar of flour will not be used up and the jug of oil will not run dry until the day the Lord gives rain on the land.'" (1 Kings 17:13–14)

The woman in this story believed she was going to make a last meal for her son and herself and then die of starvation. When asked to provide for Elijah, what did she do?

Have you ever been short on something and then someone comes and asks to borrow the little you have left? What does it feel like to have to make that kind of decision? How do you know if you made the right choice?

Ingredients:

two 8-ounce packages cream cheese

2 eggs

¾ cup sugar

1 teaspoon vanilla

cherry or blueberry pie filling

Materials Needed:

mixer

bowl

measuring cups and spoons

cupcake liners

cupcake pan

Directions:

1. Mix all ingredients except pie filling until smooth.
2. Put cupcake liners into cupcake pan.
3. Pour mixture into individual cupcake liners.
4. Bake at 375 degrees for 30 minutes for large size cupcakes and 15 minutes for small size cupcakes.
5. Chill.
6. Serve topped with fruit pie filling.

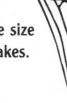

GP275508 Cooking With Christian Kids

"Trees" of the Wood Broccoli Dish

Then the trees of the forest will sing, they will sing for joy before the Lord, for he comes to judge the earth. (1 Chronicles 16:33)

When Jesus returns, the earth will rejoice, for it stands innocent before the Lord. When Jesus returns to earth, will you be able to rejoice because you stand innocent before the Lord?

Ingredients:

two 10-ounce packages frozen broccoli

½ teaspoon oregano

½ teaspoon salt

½ cup mayonnaise

¼ cup sharp processed cheese

1 tablespoon milk

Materials Needed:

pan filled with water

serving dish

measuring cups and spoons

double boiler

Directions:

1. Add oregano and salt to pan of water.

2. Cook broccoli in boiling water. Drain broccoli when tender and lay in serving dish.

3. In top of a double boiler, mix mayonnaise, cheese, and milk.

4. Heat until cheese melts and mixture is hot.

5. Pour over broccoli and serve.

GP275508 Cooking With Christian Kids

Sheba's Iced Fruit 'n' Spice Bread

. . . There had never been such spices as those the queen of Sheba gave to King Solomon. (2 Chronicles 9:9)

Spices were a thing of great value during Biblical times. Jesus was presented with spices at his birth. What gifts are given now as a gift of great value? Are they the same things God values?

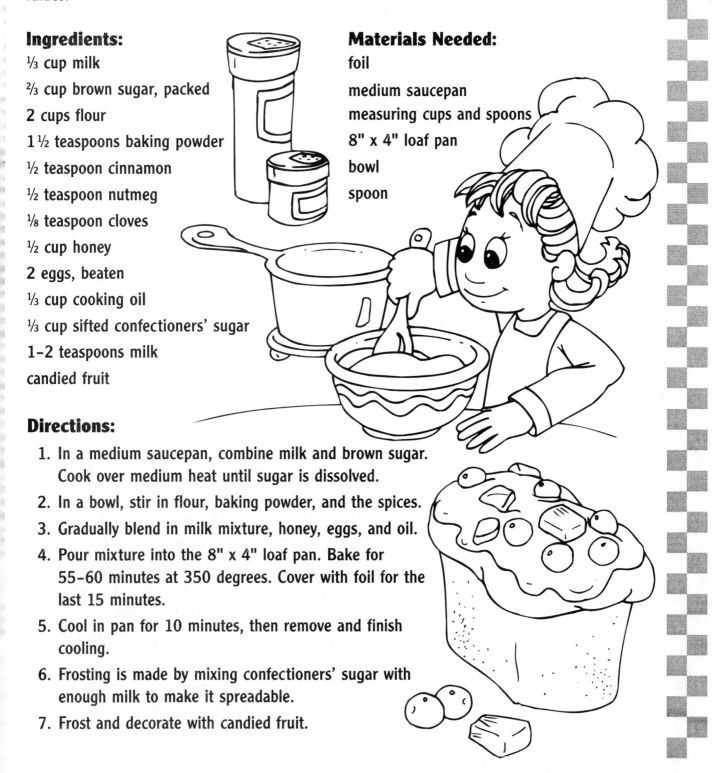

Ingredients:

⅓ cup milk

⅔ cup brown sugar, packed

2 cups flour

1 ½ teaspoons baking powder

½ teaspoon cinnamon

½ teaspoon nutmeg

⅛ teaspoon cloves

½ cup honey

2 eggs, beaten

⅓ cup cooking oil

⅓ cup sifted confectioners' sugar

1-2 teaspoons milk

candied fruit

Materials Needed:

foil

medium saucepan

measuring cups and spoons

8" x 4" loaf pan

bowl

spoon

Directions:

1. In a medium saucepan, combine milk and brown sugar. Cook over medium heat until sugar is dissolved.

2. In a bowl, stir in flour, baking powder, and the spices.

3. Gradually blend in milk mixture, honey, eggs, and oil.

4. Pour mixture into the 8" x 4" loaf pan. Bake for 55-60 minutes at 350 degrees. Cover with foil for the last 15 minutes.

5. Cool in pan for 10 minutes, then remove and finish cooling.

6. Frosting is made by mixing confectioners' sugar with enough milk to make it spreadable.

7. Frost and decorate with candied fruit.

 GP275508 Cooking With Christian Kids

Hidden Rubies Gelatin Treat

" . . . the price of wisdom is beyond rubies." (Job 28:18)

Have you ever heard *"A diamond is a girl's best friend"*? **What do you think about this saying? What would God say about this saying?**

Ingredients:

large honeydew melon

3-ounce box raspberry gelatin

¾ cup boiling water

10-ounce package frozen raspberries

¼ cup cran-raspberry juice

1 tablespoon lime juice

dash salt

Materials Needed:

pan

knife

bowls

scissors

paper cup

long-handled spoon

paper towels

Directions:

1. Cut a round plug out of the end of the melon, approximately 2½" round. Keep the plug for later use.

2. Use a long-handled spoon to remove the seeds. Turn melon upside down on paper towels to drain thoroughly.

3. Dissolve gelatin in boiling water. Add raspberries, both juices, and salt. Chill until partially set.

4. Cut the bottom out of a paper cup. This will be used as a funnel.

5. Prop melon in a bowl with the opening up. Place funnel in hole and pour gelatin mixture into melon to the top. Replace the plug.

6. Mold remaining gelatin mixture separately.

7. Chill overnight. Carefully cut the melon into wedges to serve.

GP275508 Cooking With Christian Kids

Fish of the Sea Sandwich

You made him ruler over the works of your hands; you put everything under his feet: all flocks and herds, and the beasts of the field, the birds of the air, and the fish of the sea, all that swim the paths of the seas. (Psalm 8:6–8)

God loved mankind so much that he gave the earth and all its inhabitants to mankind. He gave us responsibility. Earth and all its creatures depend on mankind for survival. How do you think you are doing as a caregiver?

Ingredients:

1 can tuna fish, packed in water

Miracle Whip™

celery

olives

submarine bun

Materials Needed:

can opener

knife

bowl

fork

Directions:

1. Carefully open the can of tuna and drain off the water. Put it into the bowl.
2. Mix in Miracle Whip™ to desired taste.
3. Cut the bun in half. Then cut the half of the bun to look like a fish.
4. Spread the tuna salad on the bun.
5. Cut the celery into thin slices. These will form the scales. Lay them on the fish body.
6. Cut the olives longways in strips. Use these to form the gills and fins.
7. Cut an olive horizontally to make an eye.

31

GP275508 Cooking With Christian Kids

Green Pastures Salad

He makes me lie down in green pastures . . .
(Psalm 23:2)

When was the last time you went out and laid down in a field of grass, smelled the wonderful smells of nature, and looked at the sky? How awesome is our God! What else do you notice as you are lying in the grass?

Ingredients:

Salad

2 large Granny Smith apples

⅛ cup lemon juice

½ teaspoon sugar

9 cups torn lettuce

Apple Cider Dressing

2 cups apple cider

½ cup apple cider vinegar

¼ cup oil

1 tablespoon Dijon-style mustard

1 tablespoon sugar

½ teaspoon salt

¼ teaspoon pepper

Materials Needed:

cutting board

measuring cups and spoons

knife

bowls

strainer

jar with a lid

spoons

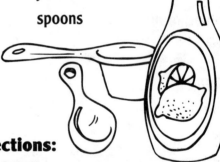

Directions:

Salad

1. Mix lemon juice and sugar.
2. Slice apples into small chunks
3. Toss juice mixture with apples.
4. Wash and drain lettuce. Tear lettuce and put it in a bowl.
5. Mix apples with lettuce.

Dressing

1. Pour all ingredients into a jar with a lid.
2. Shake to mix.
3. Serve over salad.

GP275508 Cooking With Christian Kids

Taste and See Fruit Delight

Taste and see that the Lord is good . . .
(Psalm 34:8)

God has blessed us with so many good things—delicious food, beautiful days, cozy beds at night! How many things can you think of that are examples of God's love?

Ingredients:

strawberries

blueberries

raspberries

½ cup whipping cream

1 teaspoon sugar

¼ teaspoon vanilla

Materials Needed:

strainer

mixer

bowl

spoon

parfait glass

measuring cups and spoons

Directions:

1. Wash strawberries. Remove the stems and leaves. Leave in strainer to drip dry.

2. In a bowl, mix whipping cream, sugar, and vanilla until light and fluffy.

3. Put strawberries in a parfait glass and then add whipped cream.

4. Next, put a layer of blueberries and then add a layer of whipped cream.

5. Put raspberries on last and then add a last layer of whipped cream.

6. Top with one strawberry.

GP275508 Cooking With Christian Kids

Smile, God Loves You! Apple Slices

How priceless is your unfailing love . . . (Psalm 36:7)

Love. People say the word *love* daily. "I *love* going to the movies!" "I *love* my new sweater!" "I *love* pizza!" But all of those *loves* are temporary. Here today, gone tomorrow. God's love is eternal. How does God's love make you feel?

Ingredients:
Red Delicious apples
mini marshmallows
peanut butter

Materials Needed:
cutting board
knife

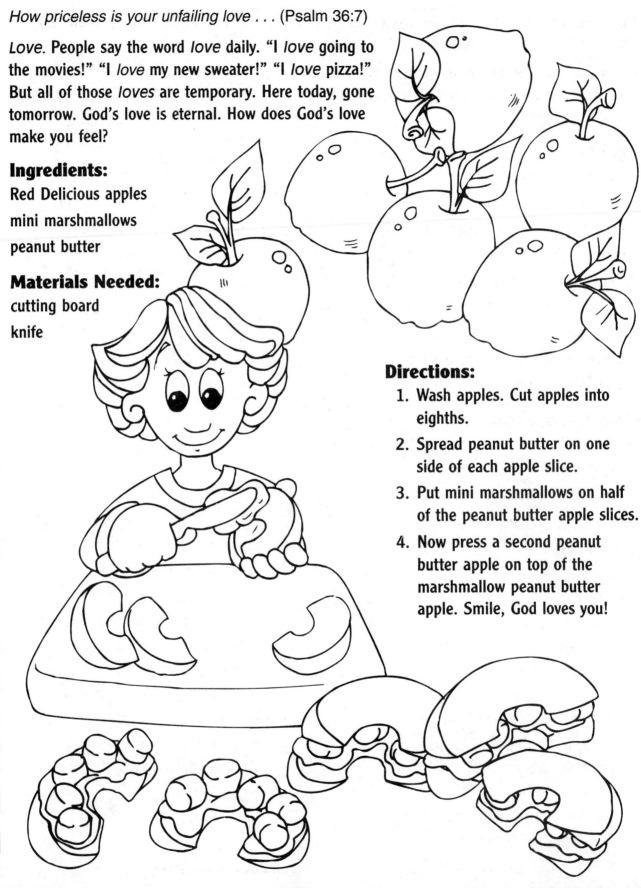

Directions:

1. Wash apples. Cut apples into eighths.

2. Spread peanut butter on one side of each apple slice.

3. Put mini marshmallows on half of the peanut butter apple slices.

4. Now press a second peanut butter apple on top of the marshmallow peanut butter apple. Smile, God loves you!

Frozen Peanut Butter Pie

His speech is smooth as butter, yet war is in his heart; his words are more soothing than oil, yet they are drawn swords. (Psalm 55:21)

It is sad to say that everyone we meet cannot be trusted. There are people whose words seem kind enough, but there is evil in their hearts. How can we protect ourselves from these kinds of people?

Ingredients:

18 graham cracker squares

¼ cup sugar

6 tablespoons melted margarine

8-ounce package cream cheese

½ cup smooth peanut butter

1 cup sifted confectioners' sugar

½ cup milk

8 ounces whipped topping, thawed

¼ cup chopped peanuts

Materials Needed:

bowls

pie pan

mixer

measuring cups and spoons

sifter

spoon

foil

Directions:

1. Crush graham crackers and put 1¼ cups of crumbs into mixing bowl.
2. Add sugar and butter and mix well.
3. Press crumb mixture into the bottom and sides of the pie pan to form a firm, even crust. Chill.
4. In large mixing bowl, beat cream cheese and peanut butter until well blended.
5. Beat in confectioners' sugar and milk.
6. Fold in the whipped topping.
7. Pour mixture into pie crust.
8. Sprinkle with nuts, cover with foil, and put in freezer until frozen.
9. Let stand at room temperature for 10 minutes before serving.

Gift Bread

You care for the land and water it; you enrich it abundantly. The streams of God are filled with water to provide the people with grain, for so you have ordained it. (Psalm 65:9)

God provided us with water to drink, land to grow crops, and fields to feed farm animals. What other gifts did God give us to help us survive? Are there any gifts he did not provide us with?

Ingredients:
½ cup cornmeal

½ cup flour

1 tablespoon honey

1 teaspoon baking powder

½ teaspoon salt

2 tablespoons shortening

1 small egg

½ cup milk

½ cup corn, at room temperature

butter and honey

Materials Needed:
bowl

spoon

measuring cups and spoons

loaf pan

non-stick spray

Directions:
1. Mix together the cornmeal, flour, honey, baking powder, and salt in the bowl.

2. Add shortening, egg, and milk. Stir until lumps are gone.

3. Stir corn into mix.

4. Spray loaf pan with non-stick spray.

5. Pour mix into loaf pan.

6. Bake at 400 degrees for 25 minutes.

7. Serve with butter and honey.

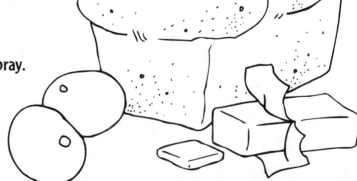

Sun Bars

For the Lord God is a sun and shield . . . (Psalm 84:11)

Without the sun, there would no life as we know it. Without God's son, there would be no life as we know it. What would your life be like without the sun/son?

Ingredients:

1 cup flour

½ cup margarine

⅓ cup confectioners' sugar

1 cup granulated sugar

3 tablespoons lemon juice

½ cup coconut

½ teaspoon baking powder

¼ teaspoon salt

2 eggs

Materials Needed:

bowl

8" square pan

measuring cups and spoons

mixer

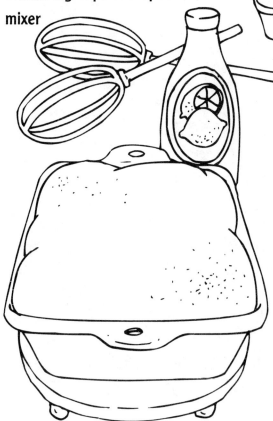

Directions:

1. Mix flour, margarine, and confectioners' sugar in a bowl. Then pour it into the square pan.

2. Flour your fingers and then press flour mixture evenly across the bottom of the pan.

3. Bake in 350-degree oven for 20 minutes.

4. Mix granulated sugar, lemon juice, baking powder, salt, eggs, and coconut until mixture is foamy.

5. Pour liquid mixture over the hot crust and put back into the oven for 25 minutes, or when the bars are firm to the touch.

6. Let cool. Dust the top with confectioners' sugar.

GP275508 Cooking With Christian Kids

Sea Foam Cookie

You rule over the surging sea; when its waves mount up, you still them. (Psalm 89:9)

Does your life ever seem to be out of control? How do you handle it when things seem to be crazy?

Ingredients:

½ cup shortening

½ cup sugar

1 ½ cups brown sugar, firmly packed

2 eggs, separated

1 teaspoon vanilla

2 cups flour

2 teaspoons baking powder

1 teaspoon baking soda

½ teaspoon salt

3 tablespoons milk

6-ounce package chocolate chips

¾ cup salted peanuts, chopped

Materials Needed:

mixer

measuring cups and spoons

bowls

9" x 13" pan

non-stick spray

spoon

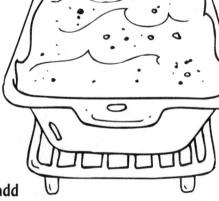

Directions:

1. In a bowl, cream shortening with white sugar and ½ cup brown sugar.

2. Beat in egg yolks and vanilla.

3. In a second bowl, mix flour, baking powder, baking soda, and salt.

4. Stir dry ingredients into creamed mixture while adding alternately with milk. (The dough will be stiff.)

5. Press mixture into the greased 9" x 13" pan.

6. Sprinkle chocolate chips over the top.

7. Beat egg whites until soft peaks form. Gradually add the remaining one cup of brown sugar and beat until firm and glossy.

8. Spread egg mixture over the dough in the pan. Sprinkle the peanuts evenly over the top.

9. Bake in a 325-degree oven, 30–35 minutes. Cool before cutting.

Fruit Frogs

Their land teemed with frogs . . . (Psalm 105:30)

David shares the history of the plagues sent to Egypt so that the Israelites would be set free. He wants everyone to know how mighty, how wonderful, and how thankful he is. David uses phrases like "Give thanks," "Sing praise," "Rejoice!"

Can you think of a time that made a difference in our history that we would still want to celebrate years later with David's same excitement?

Ingredients:

honeydew melon

3-ounce box lime gelatin

1 cup boiling water

6-ounce container plain yogurt

raisins

kiwi fruit

Materials Needed:

bowl

knife

cutting board

spoon

toothpicks

potato peeler

plates

Directions:

1. Pour gelatin into the bowl. Add hot water and stir until gelatin mix dissolves.

2. Stir in plain yogurt. Cut honeydew melon in half. Scoop out seeds using a spoon. Pat dry and set upside down to drain any extra juice.

3. Scoop gelatin mixture into melon halves. Swipe a knife across the top of the melon to remove any gelatin mixture blobs and to have a straight edge.

4. Chill until firm.

5. Peel the kiwi fruit. Cut the kiwi fruit in half. These will be the frog's eyes.

6. Cut melon halves in half, so you have 4 slices. Place them on separate plates.

7. Use toothpicks to attach the kiwi fruit for eyes. Add a raisin for a nose.

GP275508 Cooking With Christian Kids

Mac 'n' Cheese Cups

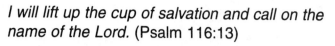

I will lift up the cup of salvation and call on the name of the Lord. (Psalm 116:13)

When you pray, what do you pray for? Do you pray about school or a fear or desire? When was the last time you called upon the Lord for your salvation? Only by recognizing Jesus as our salvation can we enter the kingdom of heaven.

Ingredients:

1 cup uncooked elbow macaroni

8 medium green peppers

2 cups cubed cooked ham

1 cup shredded sharp cheddar cheese

¼ cup diced canned pimiento

2 tablespoons finely chopped onion

½ cup mayonnaise

2 teaspoons prepared mustard

¼ teaspoon salt

lettuce leaves

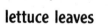

Materials Needed:

pan, knife, cutting board, plate, measuring cups and spoons, spoon

Directions:

1. Cook macaroni according to package. Drain and cool.

2. Cut off tops of peppers and remove seeds and membrane.

3. Cook peppers in boiling water for 5 minutes. Plunge immediately into cold water.

4. Combine macaroni, ham, cheese, pimiento, and onion.

5. Blend mayonnaise, mustard, and salt. Mix this in with the macaroni mixture.

6. Stuff the peppers with the macaroni mixture and chill.

7. Serve on a lettuce-lined plate.

GP275508 Cooking With Christian Kids

Vegetable Love

Better a meal of vegetables where there is love than a fattened calf with hatred.
(Proverbs 15:17)

Before God created man, he created a garden. The garden was so beautiful, he wanted to share his creation with a loved one. So God created man. Have you ever grown a garden? What does a garden need to grow?

Ingredients:

lettuce

carrots

celery

peppers

tomatoes

onions

mushrooms

your choice of salad dressing

Materials Needed:

bowl

knife

cutting board

potato peeler

salad tongs

paper towels

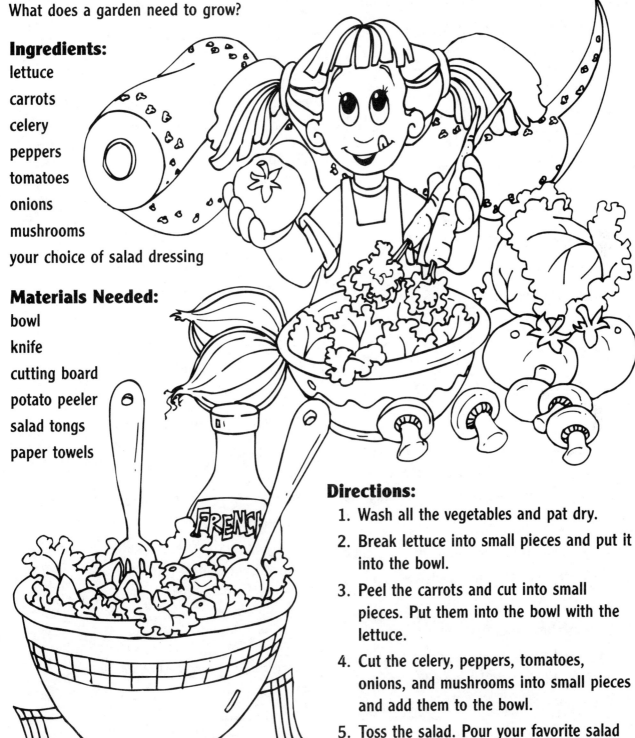

Directions:

1. Wash all the vegetables and pat dry.

2. Break lettuce into small pieces and put it into the bowl.

3. Peel the carrots and cut into small pieces. Put them into the bowl with the lettuce.

4. Cut the celery, peppers, tomatoes, onions, and mushrooms into small pieces and add them to the bowl.

5. Toss the salad. Pour your favorite salad dressing over your meal of vegetables.

Chicken Salad in the Snow

Like snow in summer or rain in harvest, honor is not fitting for a fool. (Proverbs 26:1)

Think about who you consider to be a hero—athletes who cannot control their tempers, movie stars who have loose morals, and politicians who think the law is for everyone but them. Are you honoring the wrong people? Who can you think of in your community that deserves to be honored for Christianlike behavior and service?

Ingredients:

2 envelopes unflavored gelatin

½ cup cold water

13 ¾-ounce can chicken broth

2 ½ cups cut-up, cooked chicken

1 cup mayonnaise

½ cup chopped celery

¼ cup chopped green pepper

3 tablespoons chopped pimiento-stuffed olives

2 tablespoons lemon juice

1 cup whipping cream, whipped

Materials Needed:

saucepan, spoon, 6 ½-cup gelatin mold, cutting board, knife, measuring cups and spoons, mixer, bowl

Directions:

1. Soften gelatin in cold water in a saucepan.
2. Stir over low heat until dissolved.
3. Stir in chicken broth.
4. Chill mixture until partially set.
5. Fold in chicken, mayonnaise, celery, green pepper, olives, and lemon juice.
6. Whip the whipping cream. Fold it into the mixture.
7. Pour mixture into a 6 ½-cup mold and chill until firm.

GP275508 Cooking With Christian Kids

Fig Preserves

He who tends a fig tree will eat its fruit, and he who looks after his master will be honored. (Proverbs 27:18)

Figs are mentioned many times in the Bible. If a person had a vineyard with a fig tree, he or she was thought to be living a wonderful life. What is it that makes you feel secure? How do you take care of that symbol of security?

Ingredients:

4 pounds fresh figs

1 lemon

4 cups sugar

1 cup water

biscuits or bread

Materials Needed:

knife

cutting board

pan

spoon

3-pint hot jar

measuring cup

Directions:

1. Wash and peel the figs.
2. Peel and slice the lemon.
3. Pour the sugar and the water into the pan and heat for 5 minutes.
4. Add figs and lemon to the sugar water mixture and cook rapidly until clear.
5. Pour into a 3-pint hot jar. Seal.
6. Spread on biscuits or bread and enjoy!

PAM'S FIG PRESERVES

Under the Sun Sandwich

I have seen something else under the sun: The race is not to the swift or the battle to the strong, nor does food come to the wise or wealth to the brilliant or favor to the learned; but time and chance happen to them all. (Ecclesiastes 9:11)

Just because you are a Christian does not mean that life is going to be easy. Everyone under the sun will see good times and bad. Can you think of a blessing and a disaster? What got you through the tough times?

Ingredients:

1 unsliced loaf French bread

margarine

leaf lettuce

ham

Swiss cheese, cut in half diagonally

16-ounce can peach halves, well drained

½ cup mayonnaise

2 tablespoons chili sauce

1 tablespoon pickle relish

Materials Needed:

cutting board

knife

measuring cup and spoons

Directions:

1. Cut French bread in half lengthwise (top half will not be used for this recipe).

2. Spread bread with margarine.

3. Layer lettuce, ham, cheese, and peaches on bread.

4. Mix mayonnaise, chili sauce, and pickle relish. Drizzle over the top of the sandwich.

Nourishment for the Soul Salad

Strengthen me with raisins, refresh me with apples . . . (Songs of Songs 2:5)

Food gives our bodies nourishment. Books give our brains nourishment. What gives your soul nourishment?

Ingredients:

3 apples

½ cup raisins

½ cup chopped walnuts

½ cup Miracle Whip™

¾ cup mini marshmallows

lettuce

Materials Needed:

bowl

cutting board

knife

measuring cups and spoons

spoon

serving plate

Directions:

1. Put walnuts into the bowl.
2. Add raisins.
3. Add marshmallows.
4. Wash, core, and dice the apples.
5. Add Miracle Whip™. Stir ingredients together. If too dry, add more Miracle Whip™, one tablespoon at a time.
6. Serve on a bed of lettuce.

GP275508 Cooking With Christian Kids

Curds and Honey Spread

"Therefore the Lord himself will give you a sign: The virgin will be with child and will give birth to a son, and will call him Immanuel. He will eat curds and honey when he knows enough to reject the wrong and choose the right." (Isaiah 7:14–15)

Isaiah foretold of the birth of Jesus. He also spoke of Jesus as a child growing to a young boy who could tell the difference between good and evil. Do you remember a time when you had to make a choice between doing the right thing or the wrong thing?

Ingredients:

¼ cup diced dry fruit (apples, pears, apricots, peaches)

½ cup cottage cheese

1 tablespoon milk

2 teaspoons honey

⅛ teaspoon cinnamon

bagels

Materials Needed:

cutting board

knife

blender

spatula

bowls

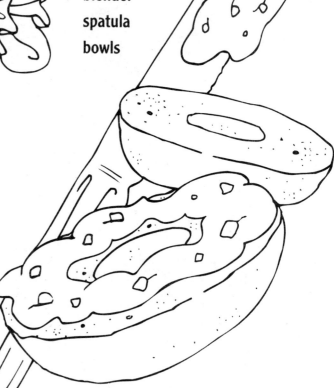

Directions:

1. Cut fruit into small pieces.
2. Pour cottage cheese, milk, honey, and cinnamon in the blender. Cover and turn on medium speed for 30 seconds.
3. Turn blender off. Scrape the sides and then turn the blender on again until mixture is smooth.
4. Scrape mixture out of blender and into another bowl.
5. Add diced fruit. Mix completely.
6. Serve on bagels.

Potter's Clay Treats

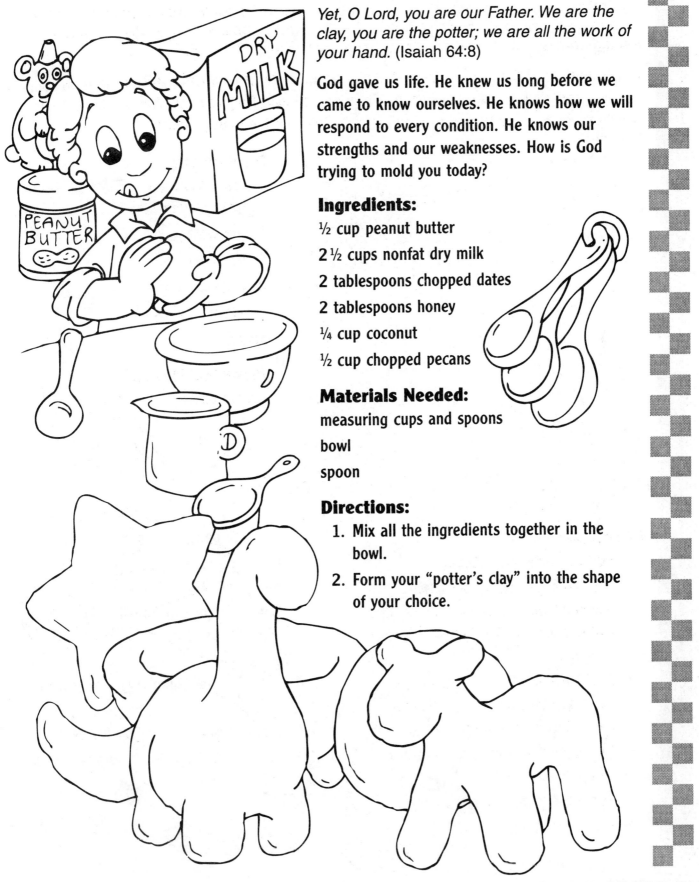

Yet, O Lord, you are our Father. We are the clay, you are the potter; we are all the work of your hand. (Isaiah 64:8)

God gave us life. He knew us long before we came to know ourselves. He knows how we will respond to every condition. He knows our strengths and our weaknesses. How is God trying to mold you today?

Ingredients:

½ cup peanut butter

2 ½ cups nonfat dry milk

2 tablespoons chopped dates

2 tablespoons honey

¼ cup coconut

½ cup chopped pecans

Materials Needed:

measuring cups and spoons

bowl

spoon

Directions:

1. Mix all the ingredients together in the bowl.
2. Form your "potter's clay" into the shape of your choice.

Daniel's Lion Fruit Snack

Daniel answered, "O king, live forever! My God sent his angel, and he shut the mouths of the lions. They have not hurt me, because I was found innocent in his sight . . . "
(Daniel 6:21–22)

Daniel didn't get eaten by the lions because of his faith in God. Can you think of a time your faith kept you out of a dangerous situation?

Ingredients:

1 pineapple slice

½ pear

raisins

maraschino cherry

apple

Materials Needed:

plate

cutting board

knife

Directions:

1. Place the pineapple slice on the plate. This will be the lion's mane.

2. Place the ½ pear in the center of the pineapple. This will be the lion's face.

3. Cut the apple into fourths. Take one slice and cut two triangles for the ears.

4. Cut the maraschino cherry in half for a nose.

5. Place raisins on the pear for eyes.

6. Slice a raisin for mouth and whiskers.

GP275508 Cooking With Christian Kids

Jonah's Whale of a Sandwich

But the Lord provided a great fish to swallow Jonah . . . (Jonah 1:17)

Can you think of a time you were disciplined by your parents, and once you had time to think about your actions, you realized your parents were right and you were wrong? As hard as it is to admit your mistakes, it is the only way we become responsible adults.

Ingredients:
pita bread

shaved turkey

lettuce

tomato

shredded cheese

mayonnaise

Materials Needed:
knife

cutting board

Directions:
1. Open a small hole in the pita for stuffing the "whale."
2. Shred the lettuce into very small pieces.
3. Cut the tomato into small pieces.
4. If you did not buy shredded cheese, cut it into little pieces.
5. Stuff the "whale's" stomach with turkey, lettuce, tomato, cheese, and mayonnaise.

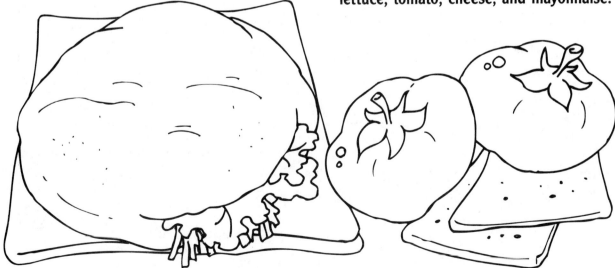

"Oh me, Oh my" Olive Spread

Though the fig tree does not bud and there are no grapes on the vines, though the olive crop fails and the fields produce no food, though there are no sheep in the pen and no cattle in the stalls, yet I will rejoice in the Lord, I will be joyful in God my Savior. (Habakkuk 3:17–18)

It is so easy to complain: "The weather is too cold (or hot)," or "I'm starving (or stuffed)." The hard thing to do is to find something to rejoice in when times get hard. Can you think of a time when you or someone you know faced a difficult time and rejoiced in the Lord? Why is it important to rejoice in times of difficulty?

Ingredients:

8-ounce package cream cheese

½ cup mayonnaise

½ cup pecans, chopped fine

1 cup salad olives, chopped

2 tablespoons olive juice

crackers

Materials Needed:

cutting board

knife

fruit jar

measuring cups and spoons

bowl

spoon

Directions:

1. Put all the ingredients into the bowl and mix. Mixture will be mushy.
2. Put the mixture into a fruit jar and refrigerate overnight or until thickened.
3. Serve as a spread for crackers.

Mount of Olives Spread

On that day his feet will stand on the Mount of Olives, east of Jerusalem, and the Mount of Olives will be split in two from east to west . . . (Zechariah 14:4)

The Mount of Olives is located east of Jerusalem. Jesus went down from here and made his triumphal entry into Jerusalem on what we celebrate today as Palm Sunday.

Zechariah is speaking of the day when all the earth and its inhabitants will be split, good from bad. Are you living a Christian life? How might you do a better job?

Ingredients:
two 8-ounce packages cream cheese

4 ounces crumbled blue cheese

1 cup shredded cheddar cheese

¼ cup minced onion

1 tablespoon Worcestershire™ sauce

green olives

minced fresh parsley

crackers

Materials Needed:
toothpicks

mixer

mixing bowl

measuring cups and spoons

cutting board

knife

Directions:
1. Put all of the cheese in the mixing bowl until it reaches room temperature.
2. Add onion and Worcestershire™ sauce.
3. Blend on low speed, then go up to medium.
4. Cover and chill overnight.
5. Shape into ball and roll in minced fresh parsley.
6. Toothpick olives all over the cheese ball. Serve with crackers.

Star Salad

. . . "Where is the one who has been born king of the Jews? We saw his star in the east and have come to worship him." (Matthew 2:2)

Stars are often used as signs of great things. Christ's birth was announced with a star. Actors are often called stars, and your teacher might give you a star for a job well done. Can you think of other symbols that represent greatness?

Ingredients:
½ cup cottage cheese

watermelon

strawberry yogurt

Materials Needed:
cutting board

knife

plate

Directions:
1. Cut watermelon into 5 equal triangles.
2. Pour the cottage cheese on a plate.
3. Place the watermelon in a star on top of the cottage cheese, leaving the center pentagon empty.
4. Pour strawberry yogurt into the center of the star, filling the pentagon.

John the Baptist's Locusts

. . . His (John the Baptist's) food was locusts and wild honey. People went out to him from Jerusalem and all Judea and the whole region of the Jordan. Confessing their sins, they were baptized by him in the Jordan River. (Matthew 3:4–6)

John the Baptist was Jesus' cousin. John's mother was Elizabeth. He was born to prepare the way for Jesus. John urged people to repent their sins and be washed clean through the waters of baptism. Have you witnessed a baptism? What was your impression of the baptism?

Ingredients:

whole dates

peanut butter

confectioners' sugar

Materials Needed:

knife

cutting board

plate

sifter

Directions:

1. Slice one side of each of the dates and remove the pits.

2. Stuff dates with peanut butter.

3. Place on a plate and sprinkle with confectioners' sugar.

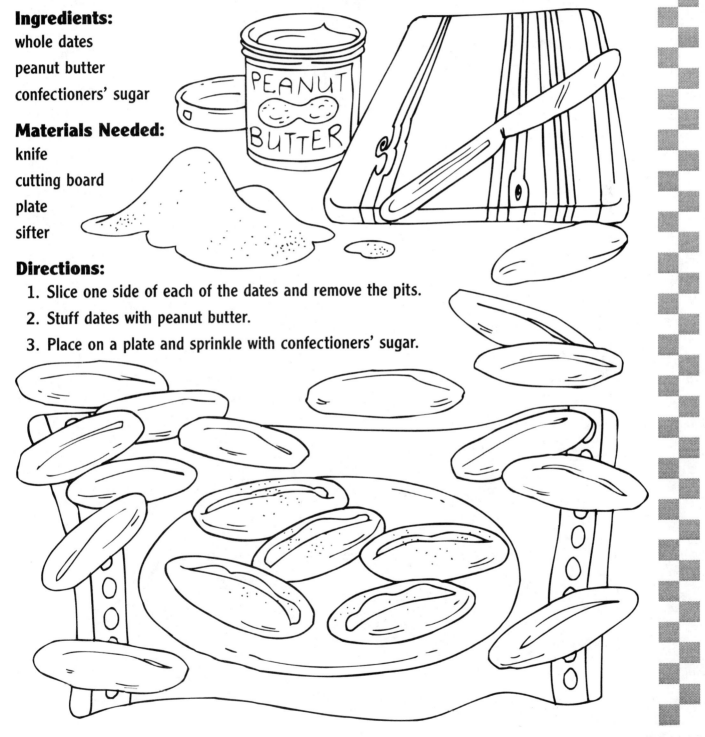

Quick Friends Salad

"Settle matters quickly with your adversary . . ." (Matthew 5:25)

Did you ever get into an argument with a friend and then because you didn't work things out right away, things kept getting worse and worse between you? What does Jesus say about settling arguments?

Ingredients:

1-pound carton cottage cheese

6-ounce box lime gelatin

8-ounce can crushed pineapple with juice

½ cup chopped nuts

large container whipped topping

Materials Needed:

can opener

bowl

measuring cup

spoon

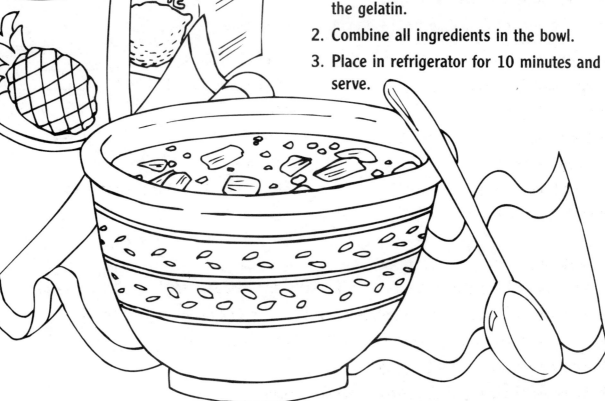

Directions:

1. Do not drain fruit. Do not add water to the gelatin.
2. Combine all ingredients in the bowl.
3. Place in refrigerator for 10 minutes and serve.

Pigs 'n' Pearls

"Do not give dogs what is sacred; do not throw your pearls to pigs . . ." (Matthew 7:6)

Your body is God's temple. He looks upon you as one of his most precious possessions. When you consider doing something not healthy for your body, like eating way too much candy or not exercising enough, you are defiling your body and God's temple. Can you think of other things that would be harmful to God's temple?

Ingredients:
¼ cup prepared mustard

1 cup currant jelly

2 tablespoons sweet pickle relish

¾ cup barbecue sauce

1 pound frankfurters

12 cocktail onions

Materials Needed:
measuring cups and spoons

knife

cutting board

saucepan

chafing dish or dish with candle warmer

spoon

Directions:
1. In a saucepan, combine mustard, jelly, relish, and barbecue sauce.
2. Heat over low heat, stirring constantly, until mixture is hot and well blended.
3. Slice frankfurters diagonally into bite-sized pieces. Add to sauce.
4. Add onions and heat thoroughly.
5. Serve from chafing dish or over a candle warmer.

Sand Tarts

"But everyone who hears these words of mine and does not put them into practice is like a foolish man who built his house on sand." (Matthew 7:26)

Jesus gave us a "plan" for living a Christian life. Where can you find the "plan?" What is the "plan?"

Ingredients:

1 cup butter

2 ¼ cups sugar

2 eggs

4 cups sifted flour

1 egg white, lightly beaten

almonds

ground cinnamon

Materials Needed:

measuring cups and spoons

bowl

mixer

rolling pin

star cookie cutter

pastry brush

cookie sheet

Directions:

1. Cream butter and sugar until light and fluffy.
2. Add eggs and flour. Mix well.
3. Chill dough thoroughly.
4. Roll dough very thin and cut with cookie cutter.
5. Brush cutout cookies with egg white and place an almond in the center of each.
6. Brush again with egg white and sprinkle with cinnamon.
7. Place cookies on an ungreased cookie sheet and bake for 5 minutes at 400 degrees.

GP275508 Cooking With Christian Kids

Fisherman's Boat Fruit Treat

Then he got into the boat and his disciples followed him. Without warning, a furious storm came up on the lake, so that the waves swept over the boat. But Jesus was sleeping. The disciples went and woke him, saying, "Lord save us! We're going to drown!"
(Matthew 8:23–25)

Have you ever been frightened? The disciples were frightened even in the company of Jesus. Jesus knew he was in God's care and that he was safe—so safe that he didn't even wake from his slumber during the storm. Jesus had faith.

Ingredients:
cantaloupe

cheese slice

grapes

strawberries

Materials Needed:
cutting board

knife

toothpicks

kabob stick

spoon

Directions:

1. Cut the cantaloupe in half. Clean out the seeds. Cut the halves into thirds. You should now have 6 slices. These will be the boats.

2. Stick a toothpick through a strawberry and into, but not through, a grape. This will be your fisherman. Stick the fisherman in the cantaloupe boat. Make as many fishermen as you desire.

3. Slice the cheese to look like a sail. Stick a kabob stick through the cheese and into the cantaloupe boat.

Buried Treasure Cookie Treats

"The kingdom of heaven is like treasure hidden in a field. When a man found it, he hid it again, and then in his joy went and sold all he had and bought that field." (Matthew 13:44)

What are the treasures in your life? What would you sacrifice to get or keep those treasures?

Ingredients:
tapioca pudding mix

fresh berries

chocolate wafer cookies

Materials Needed:
dessert cups

bowls

spoons

strainer

resealable bag

knife

paper towels

Directions:
1. Make tapioca pudding according to the directions or purchase pre-made tapioca pudding.
2. Wash berries in a strainer. Remove stems and leaves. Pat dry.
3. Put chocolate cookies in a resealable bag and seal. Crush chocolate cookies into crumbs.
4. Spread tapioca on bottom and sides of dessert cups.
5. Fill center hole with fruit (treasure).
6. Finish filling the desert cup with tapioca.
7. Sprinkle the top with chocolate cookie crumbs.

Loaves and Fishes Snack Mix

. . . Taking the five loaves and the two fish and looking up to heaven, he gave thanks and broke the loaves. Then he gave them to the disciples, and the disciples gave them to the people. They all ate and were satisfied, and the disciples picked up twelve basketfuls of broken pieces that were left over. (Matthew 14:19–20)

Jesus was faced with a hungry crowd of 5,000, having only the gift of five loaves and two fish from a young boy. Jesus blessed and broke the food into pieces. He ordered his disciples to pass the food out. When everyone had eaten, there was still plenty of food left. This was one of Jesus' many miracles.

Ingredients:

fish crackers

pretzel sticks (fat stubby type are best)

raisins and/or dried fruit

peanuts

Materials Needed:

measuring cups

bowl

resealable bags

spoon

Directions:

1. Measure two cups of fish crackers. Pour into bowl.

2. Measure two cups of pretzel sticks. Pour into bowl.

3. Measure one cup of raisins. Pour into bowl.

4. Measure one cup of dried fruit. Pour into bowl.

5. Measure one cup of peanuts. Pour into bowl.

6. Mix. Then put one cup of mix into each resealable bag. Enjoy!

Fish in a Basket Tuna Treats

They all ate and were satisfied. Afterward the disciples picked up seven basketfuls of broken pieces that were left over. (Matthew 15:37)

You are lucky enough to have plenty of wonderful food to eat. What can you do to help the hungry? How can you help the homeless?

Ingredients:

1 large can tuna fish, packed in water
½ cup mayonnaise
flat-bottomed ice cream cones
1 stalk celery
½ small onion
4 black olives without pits
paprika

Materials Needed:

can opener
measuring cups
bowl
cutting board
knife
ice cream scoop
spoon

Directions:

1. Dice celery, onions, and olives.
2. Open the can of tuna and drain off the water.
3. Mix tuna, mayonnaise, celery, olives, and onions together.
4. Scoop tuna mixture into a cone.
5. Sprinkle top with paprika. Serve immediately before cone gets soggy.

For an extra treat, top with American cheese. Put cones into muffin tin and put into oven for 3–5 minutes or until cheese melts over the top.

Faith Sandwich

". . . I tell you the truth, if you have faith as small as a mustard seed, you can say to this mountain, 'Move from here to there' and it will move . . ." (Matthew 17:20)

Have you ever seen a mustard seed? How can such a small amount of faith be strong enough to move a mountain? Have you seen faith work miracles?

Ingredients:

1 tablespoon prepared mustard

1 stick butter, at room temperature

2 tablespoons horseradish

1 teaspoon whole poppy seeds

buns

ham

Swiss cheese

Materials Needed:

bowl

mixer

foil

spoon

measuring spoons

Directions:

1. Mix mustard, butter, horseradish, and poppy seeds in a bowl.

2. Spread the mustard mixture on the top and bottom of the bun.

3. Put ham and cheese in the bun.

4. Wrap sandwich in foil.

5. Cook at 350 degrees for 15 minutes.

6. Remove from oven and let stand 5 minutes before opening.

GP275508 Cooking With Christian Kids

Vegetable Lasagna

"For I was hungry and you gave me something to eat, I was thirsty and you gave me something to drink . . ." (Matthew 25:35)

Have you ever been hot? You were probably lucky enough to be able to go somewhere cool. Think about the poor people who have nowhere to go to get out of the heat, or perhaps the cold. How can you help these people?

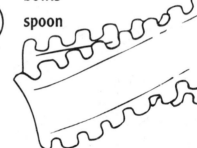

Ingredients:

1 pound fresh spinach

4 tablespoons olive oil

1 pound mushrooms, sliced

1 cup chopped onion

2 cups ricotta cheese

1 cup Parmesan cheese

3 tablespoons fresh basil, chopped

½ box lasagna noodles, cooked

2 cups shredded mixed Monterey Jack, sharp cheddar, and hot pepper cheese

Materials Needed:

8" x 8" baking pan

non-stick spray

skillet

measuring cups and spoons

bowls

spoon

Directions:

1. Wash spinach and remove tough stems.

2. Heat oil in large skillet.

3. Saute spinach, onions, and mushrooms until barely tender.

4. In separate bowl, mix ricotta, Parmesan, and basil.

5. Spray 8" square baking pan with non-stick spray.

6. Spread spinach mixture in pan. Top with half of the shredded cheese.

7. Put a layer of cooked noodles on top.

8. Top with ricotta mixture.

9. Put a second layer of noodles on top of the ricotta mixture.

10. Sprinkle on the remaining shredded cheese.

11. Bake at 350 degrees for 30 minutes.

Clouds of Heaven Meringues

"Yes, it is as you say," Jesus replied. "But I say to you: In the future you will see the Son of Man sitting at the right hand of the Mighty One and coming on the clouds of heaven." (Matthew 26:64)

So many times, clouds look so inviting—the colors, the shapes, the way the light streams down between them. Do you ever look at the sky wondering if it is God finally coming? Would you be ready?

Ingredients:
8 egg whites

2 cups sugar

shortening

flour

Materials Needed:
cookie sheet

mixer

bowl

spoon

spatula

measuring cups

wire rack

Directions:
1. Grease and lightly flour a cookie sheet. Set oven at 225 degrees.

2. Beat the egg whites in a bowl until stiff.

3. Add the sugar, a little at a time. Continue to mix, scraping the sides of the bowl until all the sugar is added.

4. Drop plump spoonfuls of the mixture onto the baking sheet.

5. Bake the meringues for 2–2½ hours until they are set.

6. Let them cool on a wire rack.

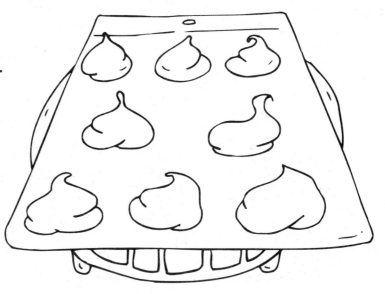

Mock Apple Pie

"We are going up to Jerusalem," he said, "and the Son of Man will be betrayed to the chief priests and teachers of the law. They will condemn him to death and will hand him over to the Gentiles, who will mock him . . . and kill him. Three days later he will rise."
(Mark 10:33–34)

What does it mean to mock someone? Have you ever witnessed someone being mocked by others? How did it make you feel? Is there something you could have done to help that person?

Ingredients:

2 refrigerator pie crusts for 9" pie pan

36 Ritz™ crackers

2 cups sugar

2 cups water

2 teaspoons cream of tartar

2 tablespoons lemon juice

grated rind of 1 lemon

¼ stick butter

cinnamon

vanilla ice cream

Materials Needed:

pie pan

measuring cups and spoons

cooking pan

knife

spoon

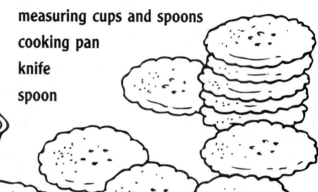

Directions:

1. Place first pie crust in pie pan.
2. Break the Ritz™ crackers into chunks and place them in the pie pan.
3. To make the syrup, pour water, sugar, and cream of tartar in a pan and boil slowly for 15 minutes.
4. Add lemon juice and rind to the syrup and let cool.
5. Pour the syrup over the crackers in the pie pan.
6. Dot with butter and sprinkle with cinnamon.
7. Cover with the second pie crust. Pinch the edges and then poke holes in the top to let the steam escape.
8. Bake at 425 degrees for 30–35 minutes until golden brown.
9. Serve with vanilla ice cream.

GP275508 Cooking With Christian Kids

Tombstone Potatoes

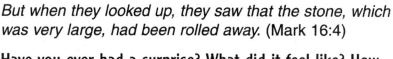

But when they looked up, they saw that the stone, which was very large, had been rolled away. (Mark 16:4)

Have you ever had a surprise? What did it feel like? How do you think the women who came to tend to Jesus felt?

Ingredients:

potatoes

milk

grated cheddar cheese

bacon bits

butter

salt

pepper

cooking oil

Materials Needed:

fork

hot pads

knife

spoon

mixer

bowl

baking dish

Directions:

1. Scrub the potatoes. Poke with fork. Rub the potatoes with cooking oil.

2. Preheat the oven to 400 degrees. Place the potatoes on the oven rack. Cook for 45–60 minutes. You will know when they are done by piercing them with a fork. If the fork goes in easily, the potatoes are done.

3. Take the potatoes out and let cool.

4. Cut each potato in half and carefully scoop the potato out of the skin and place it into a bowl. Save the skin.

5. Mix 2 tablespoons (per potato) of cheese and milk in with the potato.

6. Add a pinch (per potato) of salt and pepper.

7. Mix in a pat of butter. Put the potato mixture back into the potato skin.

8. Sprinkle with cheese and bacon bits.

9. Put each potato in a baking dish and cook at 350 degrees for 20 minutes. It is done when the cheese on top is melted.

Impossible Pie

"For nothing is impossible with God."
(Luke 1:37)

Mary was faced with the impossible, the pregnancy of our Lord. The angel Gabriel assured her that nothing is impossible with God. Mary accepted this and believed. Can you think of any other Bible figures who were told to do something impossible? Can you think of a person you know who may have been asked to do the impossible?

Ingredients:

½ cup Bisquick™

½ cup sugar

4 eggs

2 cups milk

3 ½-ounce can coconut

1 teaspoon vanilla

3 tablespoons butter

Materials Needed:

non-stick spray

9" pie pan

blender

spoon

measuring cups and spoons

Directions:

1. Put all the ingredients into the blender. Mix on medium until blended.

2. Spray the pie pan with non-stick spray.

3. Pour mixture into the pie pan.

4. Bake at 400 degrees for 25–30 minutes or until custard is set.

5. Put it into the refrigerator until chilled.

Hay in a Manger Treats

and she gave birth to her firstborn, a son. She wrapped him in cloths and placed him in a manger, because there was no room for them in the inn. (Luke 2:7)

Jesus was not born in a castle with servants and a fancy crib. Jesus was born in the most humble of places—a stable. What was it that the Christ child had that was of value?

Ingredients:

2 small packages butterscotch chips

Shredded Wheat™ cereal

Materials Needed:

pan

spoon

wax paper

Directions:

1. Melt chips over low heat.
2. Crumble Shredded Wheat™ cereal into melted chips until mixture is thick.
3. Drop by teaspoon on wax paper and cool.

Plank in Your Eye Snacks

"Why do you look at the speck of sawdust in your brother's eye and pay no attention to the plank in your own eye?" (Luke 6:41)

It is so easy to see what someone else is doing wrong and to want to tell the world on him or her. Yet, have you taken a good look at your own actions lately? What does Jesus call us to do?

Ingredients:
½ cup honey

½ cup peanut butter

1 cup nonfat dry milk

1 ½ cups dried fruit bits

Materials Needed:
bowl

mixer

spoon

wax paper

measuring cups

knife

Directions:
1. Mix honey and peanut butter together.
2. Gradually add milk.
3. Mix in fruit bits.
4. Spread out dough on wax paper and roll into a log.
5. Refrigerate until chilled.
6. To serve, cut into slices.

Rock Candy

"I will show you what he is like who . . . hears my words and puts them into practice. He is like a man building a house, who dug down deep and laid the foundation on rock . . ." (Luke 6:47–48)

Do you ever think about what it would be like to have heard the word of God right from Jesus? How do you hear the word? What are some things the word has to say to you?

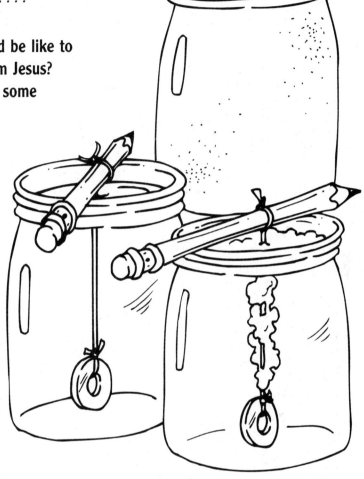

Ingredients:

sugar

water

Materials Needed:

clean large-mouth Mason jar

teapot

clean piece of white string

stainless steel washer for a weight

pencil

fork

scissors

Directions:

1. Fill the jar with sugar.

2. Bring water to a boil in a teapot. Slowly pour the water into the jar. Stop every little bit and press a fork down into the sugar so all the sugar gets wet. Continue to add water until the jar is filled. Stir until sugar is dissolved.

3. Cut a piece of string. The string should be long enough to be tied around the pencil and the washer and go from the top of the jar to the bottom of the jar.

4. Tie the piece of string to the center of a pencil. Tie a stainless steel washer to the bottom of the string.

5. Place the pencil across the mouth of the jar so the string dangles down through the sugar mixture to the bottom. Now roll the pencil so the washer is just off the bottom of the jar.

6. Set the jar, uncovered, in a warm place for a few days. Crystals will grow on the string, on the surface of the sugar mixture, and on the jar. Break the crystal surface so the water can continue to evaporate to make your rock candy!

The Widow's Coins Carrots

As he looked up, Jesus saw the rich putting their gifts into the temple treasury. He also saw a poor widow put in two very small copper coins. (Luke 21:1–2)

Are you holding back what you are willing to give to the Lord? Could you be as trusting as the widow that God will provide? Let something go today that you value. Watch what happens next.

Ingredients:

1 ½ pounds carrots

½ cup brown sugar, packed

2 tablespoons margarine

½ teaspoon salt

Materials Needed:

cutting board

knife

electric fry pan

measuring cup and spoons

potato peeler

spoon

Directions:

1. Wash and peel carrots. Cut carrots into coins.

2. Melt butter in the fry pan. Stir in the sugar and salt. Continue to cook over low heat until the mixture bubbles.

3. Add carrots. Cook and stir for about 5 minutes until carrots are glazed and cooked through.

Walk With Jesus Snack Mix

. . . "Were not our hearts burning within us while he talked with us on the road and opened the Scriptures to us?" (Luke 24:32)

When we learn God's word, we are filled with the desire to learn more. Can you think of a time that knowing God's word filled you with the desire to find out more?

Ingredients:

coconut

peanuts

sunflower seeds

raisins

carob chips

Materials Needed:

bowls

teaspoons

resealable bags

Directions:

1. Put each ingredient in a separate bowl on a long table.

2. Place a teaspoon next to each bowl.

3. Place the Bible verses below next to each bowl.

   COCONUT: *"What do you think? If a man owns a hundred sheep, and one of them wanders away, will he not leave the ninety-nine on the hills and go to look for the one that has wandered off?"* (Matthew 18:12)

   PEANUTS: *Jesus said, "Let the little children come to me, and do not hinder them, for the kingdom of heaven belongs to such as these."* (Matthew 19:14)

   SUNFLOWER SEEDS: *"For God so loved the world that he gave his one and only Son, that whoever believes in him shall not perish but have eternal life."* (John 3:16)

   RAISINS: *". . . and on the third day he will be raised to life"* . . . (Matthew 17:23)

   CAROB CHIPS: *Cast all your anxiety on him because he cares for you.* (1 Peter 5:7)

4. Give each child a resealable bag. Each child should put two teaspoons of raisins and one teaspoon of each other ingredient in his or her bag as he or she walks with Jesus.

Witness Fish Dinner

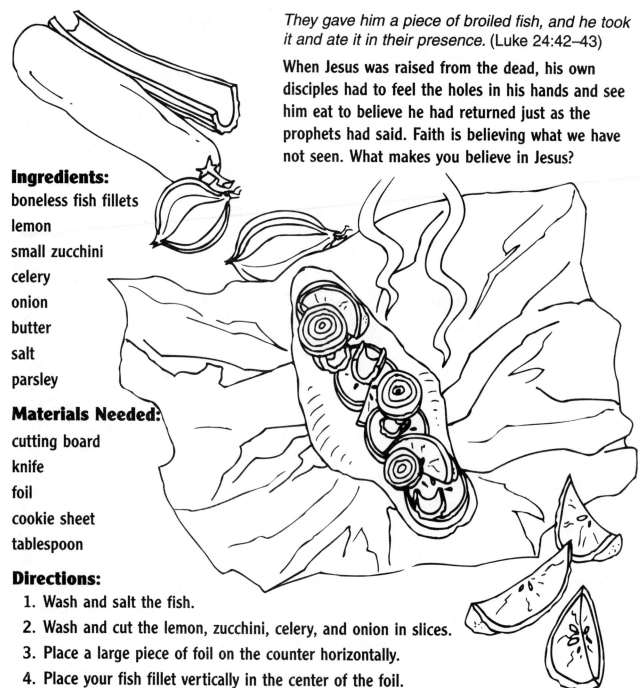

They gave him a piece of broiled fish, and he took it and ate it in their presence. (Luke 24:42–43)

When Jesus was raised from the dead, his own disciples had to feel the holes in his hands and see him eat to believe he had returned just as the prophets had said. Faith is believing what we have not seen. What makes you believe in Jesus?

Ingredients:

boneless fish fillets

lemon

small zucchini

celery

onion

butter

salt

parsley

Materials Needed:

cutting board

knife

foil

cookie sheet

tablespoon

Directions:

1. Wash and salt the fish.
2. Wash and cut the lemon, zucchini, celery, and onion in slices.
3. Place a large piece of foil on the counter horizontally.
4. Place your fish fillet vertically in the center of the foil.
5. Arrange the lemon, zucchini, celery, and onions on top of the fish.
6. Put a tablespoon of butter in the center and sprinkle with parsley.
7. Bring the right and left side of the foil to the center over the fish and roll it shut.
8. Roll the ends of the foil shut.
9. Place in a 450-degree oven, on a cookie sheet, for 15 minutes. Carefully open the foil at the end farthest from you, as the steam could burn. Fish should flake apart when pierced with a fork. If it does not look done, return it to the oven for 3–5 minutes longer.

Pizza Heaven

"In my Father's house are many rooms; if it were not so, I would have told you . . ."
(John 14:2)

What is heaven like? Is it made of marshmallow clouds and everyone gets his or her own pair of wings? How do you picture heaven?

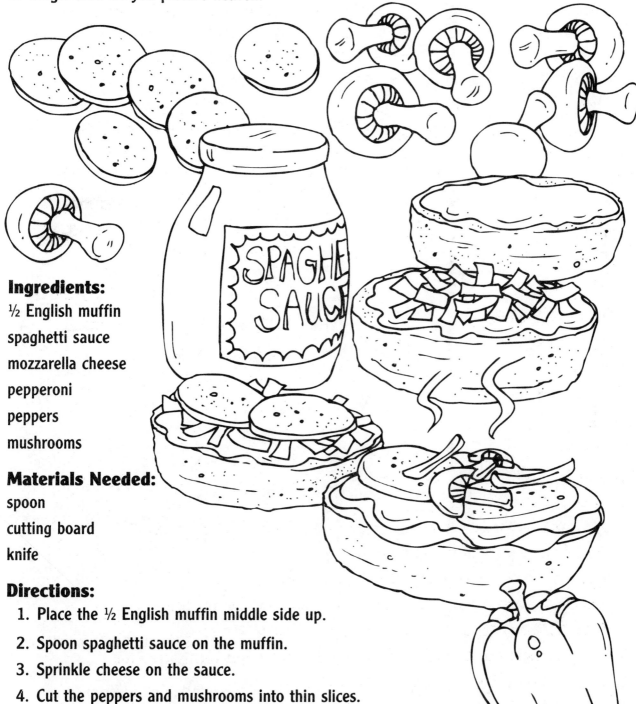

Ingredients:

½ English muffin

spaghetti sauce

mozzarella cheese

pepperoni

peppers

mushrooms

Materials Needed:

spoon

cutting board

knife

Directions:

1. Place the ½ English muffin middle side up.

2. Spoon spaghetti sauce on the muffin.

3. Sprinkle cheese on the sauce.

4. Cut the peppers and mushrooms into thin slices.

5. Place the pepperoni, peppers, and mushrooms on top of the cheese.

6. Sprinkle one last time with cheese.

7. Put into 450-degree oven for 8–10 minutes or until the cheese is melted.

GP275508 Cooking With Christian Kids

Miraculous Catch Gelatin

"I'm going out to fish," Simon Peter told them, and they said, "We'll go with you." So they went out and got into the boat, but that night they caught nothing. Early in the morning, Jesus stood on the shore, but the disciples did not realize that it was Jesus. He called out to them, "Friends, haven't you any fish?" "No," they answered. He said, "Throw your net on the right side of the boat and you will find some . . ." (John 21:3–6)

Fishing was the main source of income for several of the disciples. To come home empty-handed meant not only to go without dinner, but also to go without an income. How frustrating to know there were fish below the water and not be able to catch them! Do you ever have something important to do that cannot be completed, even when you try? Who do you turn to for help?

Ingredients:
mandarin oranges

blue gelatin

Materials Needed:
can opener

bowl

spoon

clear drink cups

Directions:
1. Open the can of mandarin oranges and drain off the juice.
2. Mix the gelatin according to the directions.
3. Pour gelatin into clear cups.
4. Drop in several "fish" (mandarin oranges).
5. Place in the refrigerator to set.

GP275508 Cooking With Christian Kids

Wonder Bars

When all the people saw him walking and praising God, they recognized him as the same man who used to sit begging at the temple gate called Beautiful, and they were filled with wonder and amazement at what had happened to him. (Acts 3:9–10)

What do you think of when you think of a thing of wonder? Can you imagine having a lifelong handicap that suddenly is lifted from you? What would be the first thing you would do?

Ingredients:

1 package blueberry muffin mix

1 package oatmeal muffin mix

1 cup pecans, chopped

16-ounce can blueberry pie filling

1 stick butter, at room temperature

Materials Needed:

can opener

9" x 13" baking pan

bowl

cutting board

knife

spoon

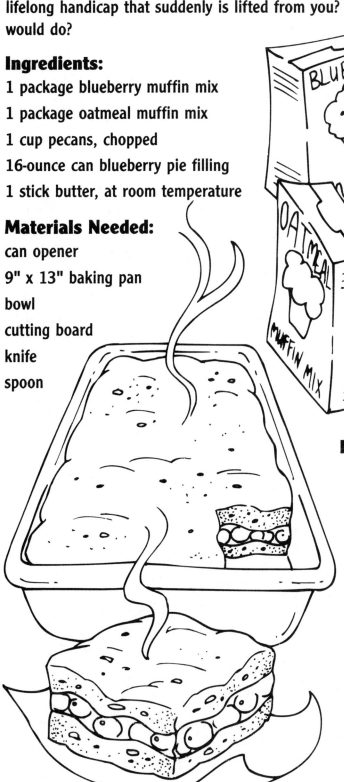

Directions:

1. Mix muffin mixes and pecans together. Add butter. Mix to get crumb mixture.

2. Spread half of the mixture over the bottom of the pan. Press down to make firm.

3. Spread blueberry pie filling over the crust.

4. Sprinkle remaining mixture over the top of the blueberry filling.

5. Bake at 350 degrees for 30–35 minutes, or until golden brown.

6. Remove from oven. Run a knife along the edges. Cut bars while still warm.

Grapes From the Vine

. . . Who plants a vineyard and does not eat of its grapes? . . .
(1 Corinthians 9:7)

God planted a seed in you long before you were born—a desire to know him. But it is not enough just to know God. God wants you to take the knowledge of him and use it in your daily life—in your actions and your speech and your choices. Can you think of a way that you have done this today?

Ingredients:
seedless grapes

granulated sugar

Materials Needed:
strainer

tray

Directions:
1. Pluck the grapes from the vine.
2. Wash the grapes and immediately roll in sugar.
3. Place the grapes on a tray. Place the tray in the freezer.
4. The grapes are ready when they are frozen.

GP275508 Cooking With Christian Kids

Raising a Raisin

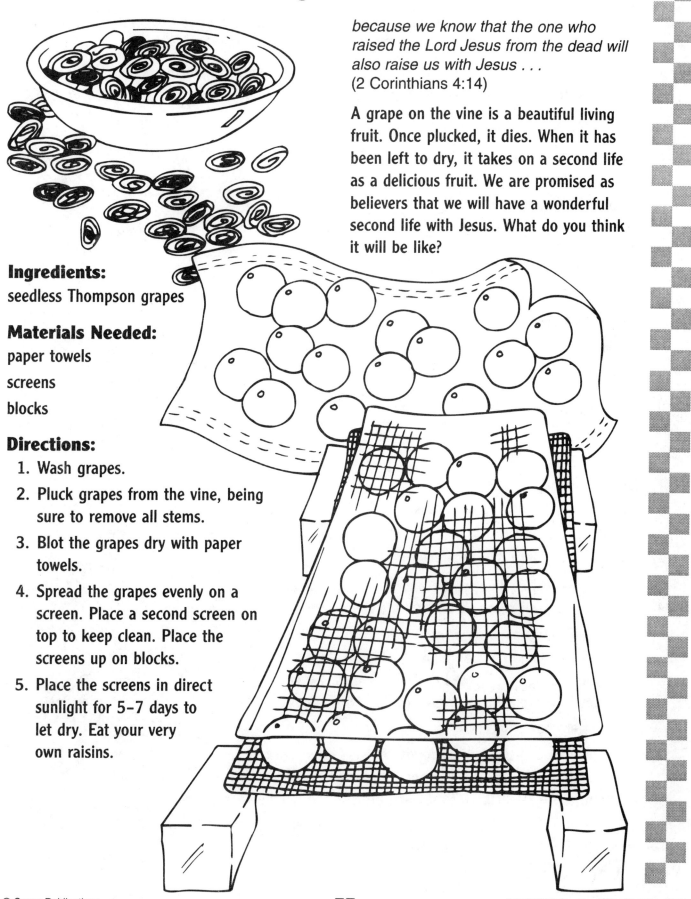

because we know that the one who raised the Lord Jesus from the dead will also raise us with Jesus . . .
(2 Corinthians 4:14)

A grape on the vine is a beautiful living fruit. Once plucked, it dies. When it has been left to dry, it takes on a second life as a delicious fruit. We are promised as believers that we will have a wonderful second life with Jesus. What do you think it will be like?

Ingredients:
seedless Thompson grapes

Materials Needed:
paper towels

screens

blocks

Directions:
1. Wash grapes.
2. Pluck grapes from the vine, being sure to remove all stems.
3. Blot the grapes dry with paper towels.
4. Spread the grapes evenly on a screen. Place a second screen on top to keep clean. Place the screens up on blocks.
5. Place the screens in direct sunlight for 5–7 days to let dry. Eat your very own raisins.

GP275508 Cooking With Christian Kids

Holy Trinity Bread

Praise be to the God and Father of our Lord Jesus Christ, who has blessed us in the heavenly realms with every spiritual blessing in Christ. (Ephesians 1:3)

Many years ago, the priests were trying to explain the holy trinity to the people. They used things like the three leaf clover and the pretzel to explain how three parts can also be one.

Ingredients:

1 ½ cups hot tap water

1 package rapid-rise yeast

⅓ cup brown sugar

3 cups flour (plus more for dusting)

coarse salt

butter

Materials Needed:

glass bowl

measuring cups

plastic wrap

two cookie sheets

spoon

Directions:

1. Preheat oven to 475 degrees.

2. Pour 1 ½ cups of the hottest water you can get from the faucet into the glass bowl.

3. Add 3 cups of flour, yeast, and ⅓ cup brown sugar to the water, stirring constantly. (Add flour until a soft dough forms.)

4. Sprinkle some flour on a clean tabletop. Take the ball of dough and knead it for 5 minutes. Cover dough with plastic wrap and let rise 10 minutes.

5. Butter cookie sheets.

6. Pinch an egg-size ball of dough off the larger ball of dough. Roll it into a long rope. Shape the dough rope into a pretzel shape with praying arms in the middle.

7. Place pretzel on cookie sheet to rise. Repeat until all the dough is formed into "Trinity Bread" (pretzels).

8. Sprinkle with salt and then bake for 8–10 minutes.

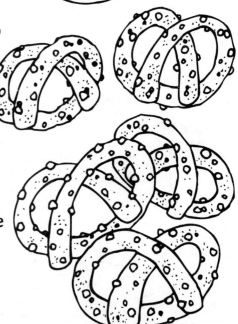

GP275508 Cooking With Christian Kids

Walls of Jericho Gelatin Treat

By faith the walls of Jericho fell, after the people had marched around them for seven days.
(Hebrews 11:30)

Have you ever been in a parade? People come to watch and see what there is to see. Can you imagine watching Joshua, 7 priests blowing trumpets, the ark of the Lord, and the guards and people marching around the walls of Jericho? What finally brought the walls down?

Ingredients:
7-ounce bottle 7-Up™

1 package lemon gelatin

1 cup hot water

½ can (16 ounces) crushed
   pineapple, drained

½ can (11 ounces) mandarin
   oranges, drained

½ cup marshmallows

Materials Needed:
bowl

measuring cups

3-cup ring mold

spoon

Directions:
1. Pour gelatin into the bowl.
2. Pour 1 cup hot water over gelatin and stir to dissolve.
3. Slowly add 7-Up™.
4. Chill until syrupy.
5. Fold in mandarin oranges, pineapple, and marshmallows.
6. Pour into a 3-cup ring mold. Chill until firm.

GP275508 Cooking With Christian Kids

Cornerstone Soup

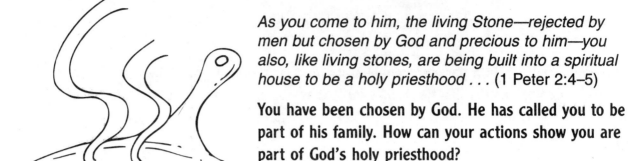

As you come to him, the living Stone—rejected by men but chosen by God and precious to him—you also, like living stones, are being built into a spiritual house to be a holy priesthood . . . (1 Peter 2:4–5)

You have been chosen by God. He has called you to be part of his family. How can your actions show you are part of God's holy priesthood?

Ingredients:

potatoes

onion

2 tablespoons butter

2 teaspoons flour

3 cups milk

salt

pepper

Materials Needed:

baking dish (microwavable)

cutting board

knife

measuring cups and spoons

spoon

fork

soup pot

Directions:

1. Wash and then poke potatoes with a fork. Put potatoes in microwave for 6–8 minutes per potato or until a fork pierces them easily. When done, let cool.

2. Dice half of one small onion.

3. In large soup pot, melt butter over stove. Add onion and let cook until onion is soft.

4. Add flour and blend.

5. Add milk. Stir until slightly thick.

6. Cut potatoes into cubes and add to the milk mixture.

7. Add salt and pepper to taste.

 GP275508 Cooking With Christian Kids